BOMB SQUAD SPECIALIST

JENNA TOLLI

PowerKiDS press

Published in 2025 by The Rosen Publishing Group, Inc.
2544 Clinton Street, Buffalo, NY 14224

Copyright © 2025 by The Rosen Publishing Group, Inc.

All rights reserved. No part of this book may be reproduced in any form without permission in writing from the publisher, except by a reviewer.

First Edition

Editor: Jenna Tolli
Book Design: Rachel Rising

Photo Credits: Cover, p. 7 dear2627/Shutterstock.com; Cover, pp. 1, 3–24 Apostrophe/Shutterstock.com; Cover, pp. 1, 3–24 ReVelStockArt/Shutterstock.com; Cover, pp. 1, 3, 4, 6, 8, 12, 16, 22–24 cobalt88/Shutterstock.com; p. 5 robert coolen/Shutterstock.com; p. 9 R R/Shutterstock.com; p. 10 Berkomaster/Shutterstock.com; p. 11 Sendo Serra/Shutterstock.com; p. 13 Katarzyna Mazurowska/Shutterstock.com; p. 15 Gorodenkoff/Shutterstock.com; p. 16 Supamotionstock.com/Shutterstock.com; p. 17 Steve Sanchez Photos/Shutterstock.com; p. 18 Matt Gush/Shutterstock.com; p. 19 photosounds/Shutterstock.com; p. 20 ANDRI TRI PUTRA/Shutterstock.com; p. 21 MilanTomazin/Shutterstock.com.

Library of Congress Cataloging-in-Publication Data

Names: Tolli, Jenna, author.
Title: Bomb squad specialist / Jenna Tolli.
Description: Buffalo : PowerKids Press, [2025] | Series: Risky jobs | Includes bibliographical references and index.
Identifiers: LCCN 2024006203 (print) | LCCN 2024006204 (ebook) | ISBN 9781499446104 (library binding) | ISBN 9781499446098 (paperback) | ISBN 9781499446111 (ebook)
Subjects: LCSH: Bomb squads–Juvenile literature. | Police–Vocational guidance–Juvenile literature.
Classification: LCC HV8080.B65 T65 2025 (print) | LCC HV8080.B65 (ebook) | DDC 363.2/3–dc23/eng/20240214
LC record available at https://lccn.loc.gov/2024006203
LC ebook record available at https://lccn.loc.gov/2024006204

Manufactured in the United States of America

Some of the images in this book illustrate individuals who are models. The depictions do not imply actual situations or events.

CPSIA Compliance Information: Batch #CSPK25. For Further Information contact Rosen Publishing at 1-800-237-9932.

CONTENTS

BOMB SQUAD SPECIALISTS 4

BECOMING AN EXPERT 6

FINDING THE DANGER.......... 8

TAKING APART A BOMB 10

CALLING IN THE BOMB SQUAD.. 12

EXPLOSIVE ORDNANCE
DISPOSAL 14

CIVILIAN BOMB SQUADS........ 16

A DANGEROUS JOB 18

KEEPING US SAFE.............. 20

GLOSSARY.................... 22

FOR MORE INFORMATION 23

INDEX 24

BOMB SQUAD SPECIALISTS

Bombs are devices that explode, or blow up. They can hurt people and damage, or harm, buildings. They can even destroy them. Bombs have explosive **materials** inside of them.

A bomb squad **specialist** is someone trained to handle bombs and make them safe for people who are around them. They need to decide how to take care of the bomb in the safest way possible.

Sometimes criminals put bombs or other explosives in a public place to hurt people. The police might find a bomb or receive a call when someone finds one. This is when the bomb squad, or team, gets called to assist.

DANGER!

Only trained professionals, or workers, should touch or move a possible bomb or explosive device. People should always call the police to report **suspicious** items. Bomb squads will come to help.

! When people hear there might be a bomb nearby, it is very scary. Bomb squads travel to the scene to quickly handle the **threat**.

5

BECOMING AN EXPERT

Bomb squad specialists know how to take bombs apart and stop them from exploding. They go to the Hazardous Devices School for training to become **experts**. This is led by the Federal Bureau of Investigation (FBI).

Part of their training takes place in a fake village on the FBI campus. It has fake movie theaters, malls, classrooms, and other places that look real. These are places where bomb threats could happen in real life. People practice what to do in different situations. Bomb squad specialists need to renew their training every three years. This helps them stay up to date with new **technology**.

DANGER!

Bomb squad specialists need to wear special suits. The suits have materials inside to protect their wearer if a bomb explodes. These suits weigh 80 pounds (36.3 kg) or more!

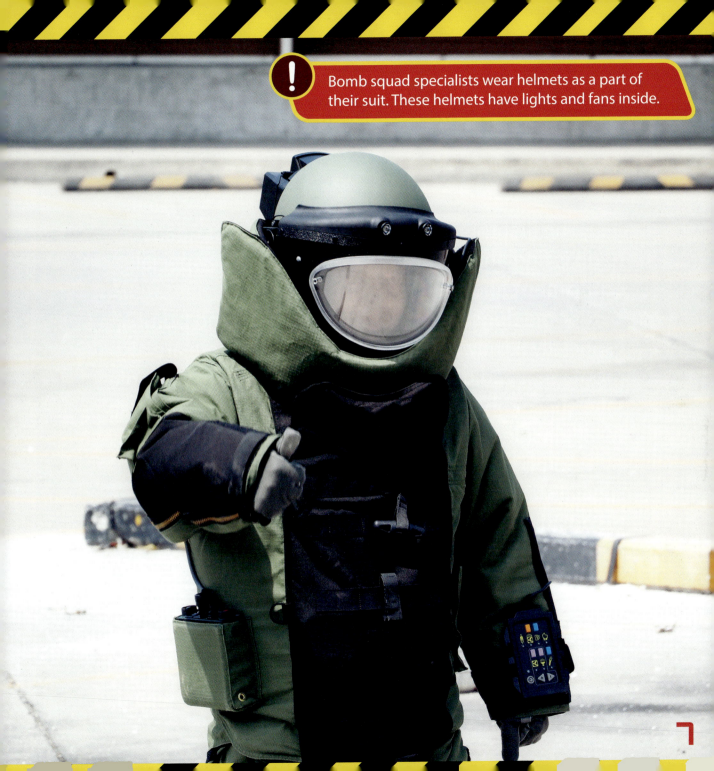

! Bomb squad specialists wear helmets as a part of their suit. These helmets have lights and fans inside.

FINDING THE DANGER

The first thing a bomb squad specialist needs to do is find and secure the bomb. They use special **equipment** and tools to do this.

Some dogs are trained to smell and find bombs, especially if they aren't out in the open. There are also robots that can **disarm** a bomb while keeping people safe. These robots can also take X-rays and help to see what's inside a bomb.

Bomb trucks are used to protect bomb squad specialists on the job. These trucks carry bomb **disposal** equipment and can hold the tools specialists may need.

DANGER!
If someone says they will detonate, or blow up, a bomb in a certain place, it's called a bomb threat. Making a bomb threat of any kind is illegal.

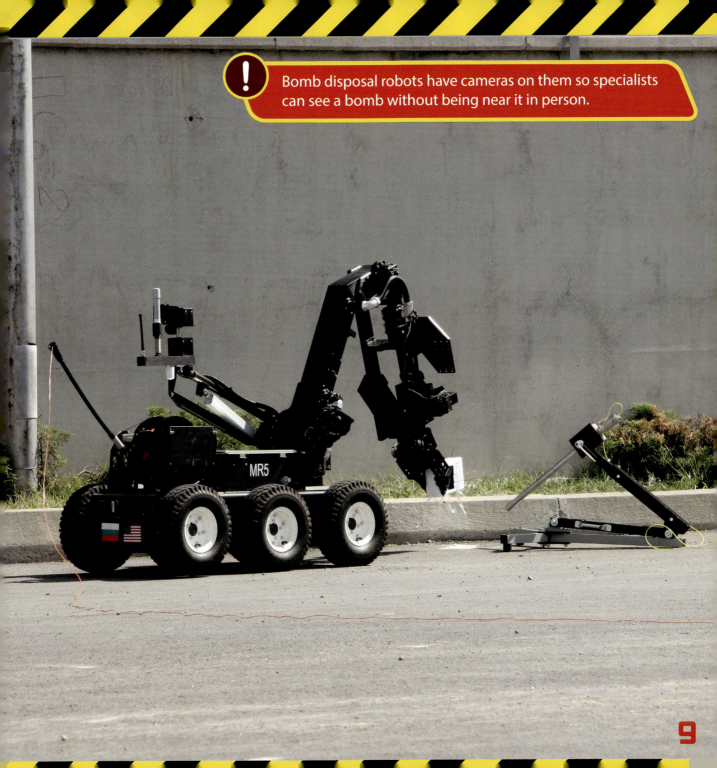
Bomb disposal robots have cameras on them so specialists can see a bomb without being near it in person.

TAKING APART A BOMB

Bombs might need to be dismantled, or taken apart. Bomb technicians can use their own hands or robots to do this. This is a stressful, or anxious, situation and can take a long time. If they make a mistake, they could hurt themselves or people around them.

Bombs can sometimes be detonated remotely. This means a robot or another piece of equipment is used while the person operating it is far away. The bomb squad first needs to get everyone away from the bomb or move it to a safe location. Then they can use their own explosives to set it off in a safer place.

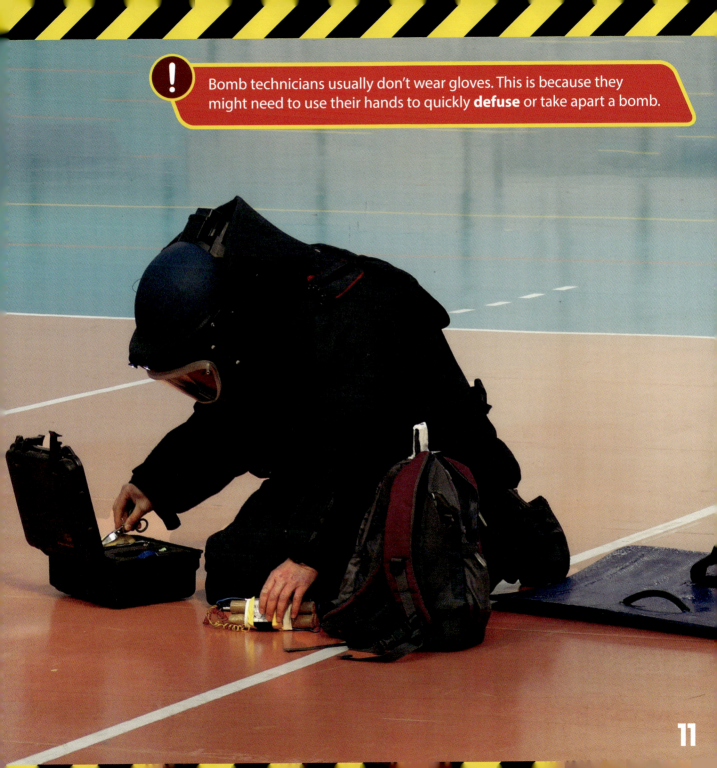

! Bomb technicians usually don't wear gloves. This is because they might need to use their hands to quickly **defuse** or take apart a bomb.

CALLING IN THE BOMB SQUAD

SWAT teams and police officers may call in the bomb squad to help them. SWAT teams handle the most dangerous types of situations. They help rescue hostages, or people who are illegally being held by force by someone else. Some criminals will hold hostages inside a building and say they have a bomb. SWAT teams work to free the hostages, and bomb squad specialists **investigate** the bomb.

Bomb squads know a lot about explosives from their training and experience. When there is a bomb at a crime scene, a bomb squad specialist can give the police more information about it.

DANGER!
Not every police department has its own bomb squad. Some bomb squads travel throughout their state to respond, or go, to emergencies and threats in different areas.

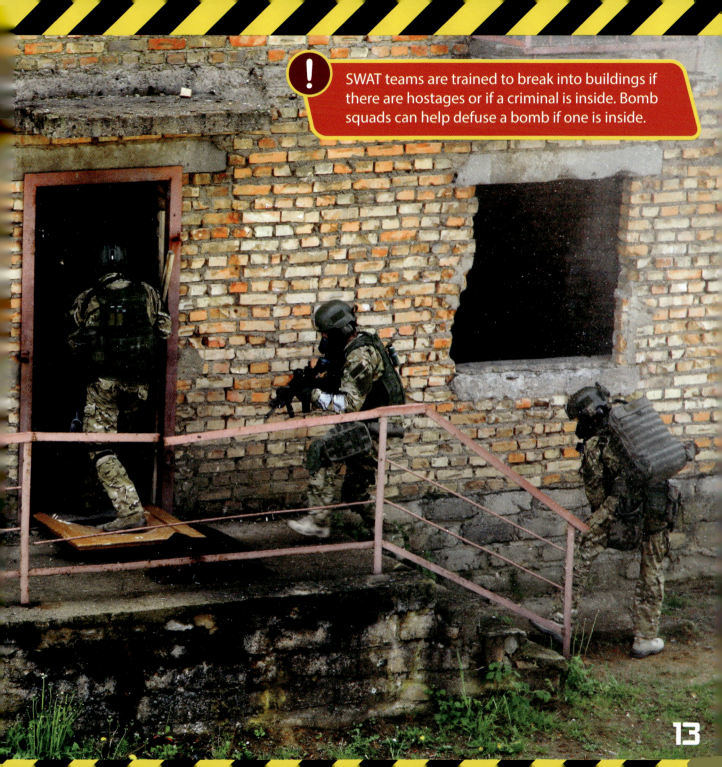

! SWAT teams are trained to break into buildings if there are hostages or if a criminal is inside. Bomb squads can help defuse a bomb if one is inside.

13

EXPLOSIVE ORDNANCE DISPOSAL

There are military bomb squads who serve in the U.S. Army, Marines, Navy, and Air Force. They are called Explosive **Ordnance** Disposal troops, or EODs. EODs work all over the world to find and disarm different kinds of bombs and weapons. They are trained to handle all kinds of bombs, including land mines, bombs that people illegally make at home, and other explosives.

Bombs can be disguised, or hidden, as different kinds of items, like packages. Bombs can also be hidden inside vests, mailboxes, or cars. EODs need to be ready for anything and make fast decisions on where a bomb could be.

! Military bomb squads started during World War II. There was a growing need to teach soldiers how to safely handle bombs.

15

CIVILIAN BOMB SQUADS

There are also civilian bomb squad specialists, such as police officers or firefighters, who are trained to handle bombs. A civilian is someone who doesn't serve in the military. These teams will be called first if there is a bomb threat in their area.

Bomb squads need to respond to the scene quickly to investigate suspicious packages and bombs. Sometimes they find active bombs that could go off at any moment and need to be disarmed. They might also be called to look at a bomb that no longer works or one that has already exploded.

DANGER!
Bomb squads can also be called in to get rid of illegal fireworks. These can explode by mistake. Bomb squads are trained to dispose of them safely.

In this photo, the New York Police Department (NYPD) bomb squad was called to look at a suspicious package inside a building.

A DANGEROUS JOB

Handling bombs and explosives is a very dangerous and risky job. If a bomb explodes before it can be disarmed, people can get injured, or hurt, or even killed.

Bomb squad specialists put themselves in danger to help protect the lives of others. Those who have lost their lives are remembered with honor and respect for their service.

The U.S. military built the EOD Memorial at Eglin Air Force Base Reserve in Niceville, Florida, to honor lost service members. You can also see a virtual memorial on the EOD Warrior Foundation's website at eodwarriorfoundation.org.

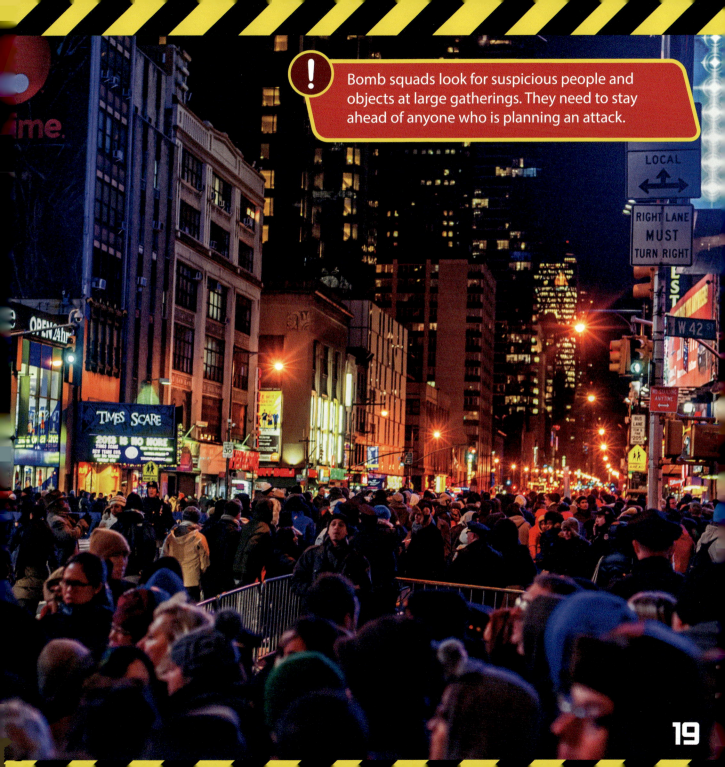
Bomb squads look for suspicious people and objects at large gatherings. They need to stay ahead of anyone who is planning an attack.

KEEPING US SAFE

To become a bomb squad specialist, you need to be very brave. You also need to be able to handle stressful and scary situations while making fast decisions. People who enjoy learning how explosives work might be interested in this job. Since bomb squads also use technology like robots and X-rays to handle bombs, working with electronics is another important skill to have.

Bomb squad specialists often find their work exciting and rewarding. Since they are experts in their field, they can help keep people safe in some of the most dangerous situations.

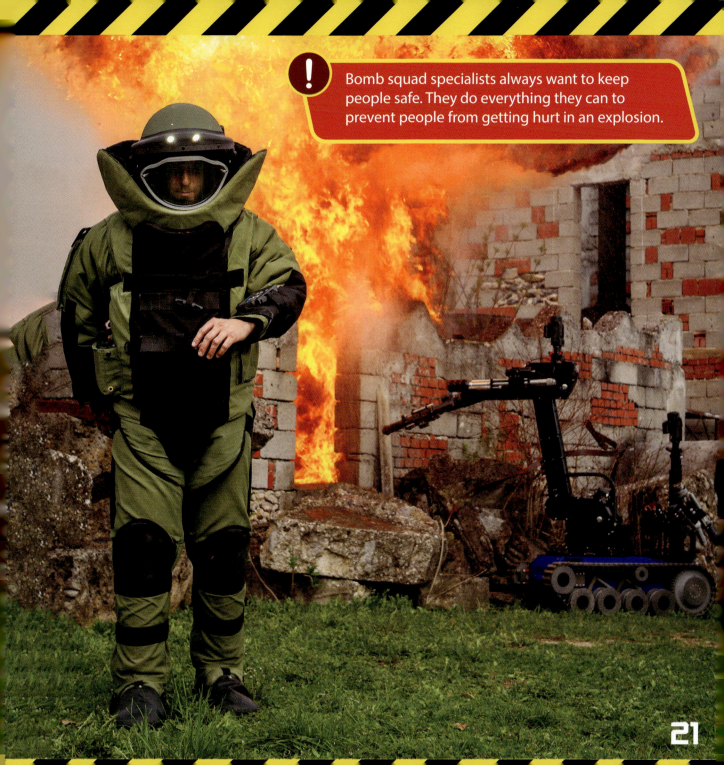

! Bomb squad specialists always want to keep people safe. They do everything they can to prevent people from getting hurt in an explosion.

GLOSSARY

defuse: To remove the fuse from something.

disarm: To make something harmless.

disposal: The act of leaving or getting rid of something.

equipment: Supplies or tools needed for a certain purpose.

expert: Someone who has a special skill or knowledge.

investigate: To study by closely examining.

material: Something from which something else can be made.

ordnance: Military supplies, including weapons.

specialist: A person who is an expert in a particular occupation, practice, or field of study.

suspicious: Causing a feeling that something is wrong.

technology: A method that uses science to solve problems and the tools used to solve those problems.

threat: Someone or something that may cause harm.

FOR MORE INFORMATION

BOOKS

Bell, Samantha. *Bomb Squad Technician: 12 Things to Know*. Mankato, MN: 12-Story Library, 2022.

Petersen, Justin. *Bomb Disposal Units: Disarming Deadly Explosives*. North Mankato, MN: Capstone Press, 2021.

WEBSITES

Cybersecurity and Infrastructure Security Agency
www.cisa.gov/bomb-threats
Learn about what steps people should take if they hear about a bomb threat.

FBI: See How We Train, Investigate Cases, and Work in Communities
www.fbi.gov/how-we-can-help-you/students
Read about what the FBI does and learn how to stay safe.

Publisher's note to educators and parents: Our editors have carefully reviewed these websites to ensure that they are suitable for students. Many websites change frequently, however, and we cannot guarantee that a site's future contents will continue to meet our high standards of quality and educational value. Be advised that students should be closely supervised whenever they access the internet.

INDEX

D

dogs, 8

E

equipment, 8, 9, 10

Explosive Ordnance
Disposal (EOD), 14, 18

F

Federal Bureau of
Investigation (FBI), 6

H

Hazardous Devices School, 6

helmets, 7

hostages, 12, 13

M

military, 14, 15, 18

P

police, 4, 12, 16, 17

R

robots, 8, 9, 10, 20

S

SWAT teams, 12, 13

T

technology, 6, 20

training, 6, 8, 12

W

World War II, 15

X

X-rays, 8, 20